Library of Congress Cataloging-in-Publication Data

Wade, L. G., (date)
   Organic chemistry/L. G. Wade, Jr.—2nd. ed.
     p.   cm.
   Includes index.
   ISBN 0-13-642588-7 :
   1. Chemistry, Organic. I. Title.
QD251.2.W33 1991
547—dc20

90-44281
CIP

Acquisitions Editor: Dan Joraanstad
Editorial/production supervision: Debra Wechsler
Interior and cover design: Margaret Kenselaar
Prepress buyer: Paula Massenaro
Manufacturing buyer: Lori Bulwin
Page layout: Carol Ann Hyland

COVER PHOTOGRAPH
A computer-generated section of a DNA molecule; blue indicates nitrogen; white, carbon;
red, oxygen; and yellow, phosphorus. The image is courtesy of Evans and Sutherland
Computer Corporation.

Printed in the United States of America

10 9 8 7 6 5 4 3 2 1

ISBN 0-13-642588-7

Prentice-Hall International (UK) Limited, *London*
Prentice-Hall of Australia Pty. Limited, *Sydney*
Prentice-Hall Canada Inc., *Toronto*
Prentice-Hall Hispanoamericana, S.A., *Mexico*
Prentice-Hall of India Private Limited, *New Delhi*
Prentice-Hall of Japan, Inc., *Tokyo*
Simon & Schuster Asia Pte. Ltd., *Singapore*
Editora Prentice-Hall do Brasil, Ltda., *Rio de Janeiro*

COMMON ABBREVIATIONS USED IN ORGANIC CHEMISTRY

ORGANIC GROUPS

Abbreviation	Meaning	Structure
Ac	acetyl	$CH_3-\overset{\overset{\displaystyle O}{\|\|}}{C}-R$
	allyl	$H_2C{=}CH{-}CH_2{-}R$
Bz	benzoyl	$Ph-\overset{\overset{\displaystyle O}{\|\|}}{C}-R$
Boc	*t*-butyloxycarbonyl	$(CH_3)_3C-O-\overset{\overset{\displaystyle O}{\|\|}}{C}-R$
Bn	benzyl	$Ph-CH_2-R$
n-Bu	*n*-butyl	$CH_3-CH_2-CH_2-CH_2-R$
i-Bu	isobutyl	$(CH_3)_2CH-CH_2-R$
s-Bu	*sec*-butyl	$CH_3-CH_2-\underset{\underset{\displaystyle CH_3}{\|}}{CH}-R$
t-Bu	*tert*-butyl	$(CH_3)_3C-R$
Cbz (or Z)	benzyloxycarbonyl	$Ph-CH_2-O-\overset{\overset{\displaystyle O}{\|\|}}{C}-R$
Me	methyl	CH_3-R
Et	ethyl	CH_3-CH_2-R
c-Hx	cyclohexyl	cyclohexyl—R
Ph	phenyl	phenyl—R
Pr	propyl	$CH_3-CH_2-CH_2-R$
i-Pr	isopropyl	$(CH_3)_2CH-R$
Sia	*secondary* isoamyl	$(CH_3)_2CH-\underset{\underset{\displaystyle CH_3}{\|}}{CH}-R$
THP	tetrahydropyranyl	tetrahydropyranyl—R
Ts	*para*-toluenesulfonyl, "tosyl"	$CH_3{-}\!\!\!\bigcirc\!\!\!{-}\overset{\overset{\displaystyle O}{\|\|}}{\underset{\underset{\displaystyle O}{\|\|}}{S}}-R$

*Not all of these abbreviations are used in this text, but they are provided
for reference.*

REAGENTS AND SOLVENTS

Abbreviation	Meaning	Structure
Ac₂O	acetic anhydride	$CH_3-\overset{\overset{\displaystyle O}{\|\|}}{C}-O-\overset{\overset{\displaystyle O}{\|\|}}{C}-CH_3$
DCC	dicyclohexylcarbodiimide	$\bigcirc\!{-}N{=}C{=}N{-}\!\bigcirc$
DIBAL or DIBAH	diisobutylaluminum hydride	$[(CH_3)_2CHCH_2]_2AlH$
DME, "glyme"	1,2-dimethoxyethane	$CH_3-O-CH_2CH_2-O-CH_3$
diglyme	bis(2-methoxyethyl) ether	$(CH_3-O-CH_2CH_2)_2O$
DMF	dimethylformamide	$H-\overset{\overset{\displaystyle O}{\|\|}}{C}-N(CH_3)_2$
DMSO	dimethyl sulfoxide	$CH_3-\overset{\overset{\displaystyle O}{\|\|}}{S}-CH_3$
EtOH	ethanol	CH_3CH_2OH
EtO⁻	ethoxide ion	$CH_3CH_2-O^-$
Et₂O	diethyl ether	$CH_3CH_2-O-CH_2CH_3$
HMPA, HMPT	hexamethylphosphoric triamide	$[(CH_3)_2N]_3P{=}O$
LAH	lithium aluminum hydride	$LiAlH_4$
LDA	lithium diisopropylamide	$[(CH_3)_2CH]_2N-Li$
MCPBA	*meta*-chloroperoxybenzoic acid	$\underset{Cl}{\bigcirc}\!\!-\overset{\overset{\displaystyle O}{\|\|}}{C}-O-O-H$
MeOH	methanol	CH_3OH
MeO⁻	methoxide ion	CH_3-O^-
MVK	methyl vinyl ketone	$CH_3-\overset{\overset{\displaystyle O}{\|\|}}{C}-CH{=}CH_2$
NBS	*N*-bromosuccinimide	(succinimide)N—Br
PCC	pyridinium chlorochromate	$pyr{\cdot}CrO_3{\cdot}HCl$
Pyr	pyridine	pyridine
t-BuOH	*tertiary* butyl alcohol	$(CH_3)_3C-OH$
t-BuOK	potassium *tertiary*-butoxide	$(CH_3)_3C-O^- {}^+K$
THF	tetrahydrofuran	tetrahydrofuran
TMS	tetramethylsilane	$(CH_3)_4Si$

L. G. WADE,

WH

ORGANI
CHEMISTR

SECOND EI

PRENTICE HALL, ENGLEWOOD CLIFFS, NEW JER!

To
Betsy,
Christine,
and Jennifer

BRIEF CONTENTS

1   INTRODUCTION AND REVIEW   1

2   STRUCTURE AND PROPERTIES OF ORGANIC MOLECULES   37

3   STRUCTURE AND STEREOCHEMISTRY OF ALKANES   78

4   THE STUDY OF CHEMICAL REACTIONS   122

5   ALKYL HALIDES: NUCLEOPHILIC SUBSTITUTION AND ELIMINATION   164

6   STEREOCHEMISTRY   223

7   STRUCTURE AND SYNTHESIS OF ALKENES   277

8   REACTIONS OF ALKENES   313

9   STRUCTURE AND SYNTHESIS OF ALCOHOLS   364

10   REACTIONS OF ALCOHOLS   401

11   INFRARED SPECTROSCOPY AND MASS SPECTROMETRY   444

12   NUCLEAR MAGNETIC RESONANCE SPECTROSCOPY   490

13   ETHERS AND EPOXIDES   559

14   ALKYNES   592

15   CONJUGATED SYSTEMS, ORBITAL SYMMETRY, AND ULTRAVIOLET SPECTROSCOPY   629

16   AROMATIC COMPOUNDS   672

17   REACTIONS OF AROMATIC COMPOUNDS   715

18   KETONES AND ALDEHYDES   767

19   AMINES   823

20   CARBOXYLIC ACIDS   887

21   CARBOXYLIC ACID DERIVATIVES   926

22   ADDITIONS AND CONDENSATIONS OF ENOLS AND ENOLATE IONS   984

23   CARBOHYDRATES AND NUCLEIC ACIDS   1043

24   AMINO ACIDS, PEPTIDES, AND PROTEINS   1101

25   LIPIDS   1146

26   SYNTHETIC POLYMERS   1166

APPENDICES   1187

ANSWERS TO SELECTED PROBLEMS   1204

INDEX   1213

CONTENTS

PREFACE xvii

1 INTRODUCTION AND REVIEW   1

1-1	The Origins of Organic Chemistry	1
1-2	Principles of Atomic Structure	2
1-3	Bond Formation: The Octet Rule	6
1-4	Lewis Structures	7
1-5	Multiple Bonding	8
1-6	Electronegativity and Bond Polarity	9
1-7	Formal Charges	10
1-8	Ionic Structures	12
1-9	Resonance Structures	13
1-10	Structural Formulas	16
1-11	Molecular Formulas and Empirical Formulas	19
1-12	Arrhenius Acids and Bases	21
1-13	Brønsted-Lowry Acids and Bases	22
1-14	Lewis Acids and Bases	27

2 STRUCTURE AND PROPERTIES OF ORGANIC MOLECULES   37

2-1	Wave Properties of Electrons in Orbitals	37
2-2	Molecular Orbitals	39
2-3	Pi Bonding	42
2-4	Hybridization and Molecular Shapes	43
2-5	Drawing Three-Dimensional Molecules	47
2-6	General Rules of Hybridization and Geometry	48
2-7	Rotation of Single Bonds	51
2-8	Rigidity of Double Bonds	52
2-9	Structural Isomerism	53
2-10	Stereoisomerism	53
2-11	Polarity of Bonds and Molecules	55
2-12	Intermolecular Attractions and Repulsions	57
2-13	Polarity Effects on Solubilities	61
2-14	Hydrocarbons	64
2-15	Organic Compounds Containing Oxygen	67
2-16	Organic Compounds Containing Nitrogen	70

3 STRUCTURE AND STEREOCHEMISTRY OF ALKANES

78

3-1 Classification of Hydrocarbons (Review) 78
3-2 Molecular Formulas of Alkanes 79
3-3 Physical Properties of Alkanes 80
3-4 Uses and Sources of Alkanes 82
3-5 Nomenclature of Alkanes 84
3-6 Structure and Conformations of Alkanes 91
3-7 Conformations of Butane 95
3-8 Conformations of Higher Alkanes 97
3-9 Cycloalkanes 97
3-10 Geometric Isomerism in Cycloalkanes 99
3-11 Stabilities of Cycloalkanes; Ring Strain 100
3-12 Cyclohexane Conformations 103
3-13 Conformations of Monosubstituted Cyclohexanes 106
3-14 Conformations of Disubstituted Cyclohexanes 109
3-15 Bicyclic Molecules 113
3-16 Reactions of Alkanes 115

4 THE STUDY OF CHEMICAL REACTIONS

122

4-1 Introduction 122
4-2 The Chlorination of Methane 122
4-3 The Free-Radical Chain Reaction 124
4-4 Equilibrium Constants and Free Energy 128
4-5 Enthalpy and Entropy 130
4-6 Bond Dissociation Energies 132
4-7 Calculation of Enthalpy Changes in Chlorination 132
4-8 Kinetics and the Rate Equation 134
4-9 Activation Energy and the Temperature Dependence of Rates 136
4-10 Transition States 138
4-11 Rates of Multistep Reactions 140
4-12 Isotope Effects 140
4-13 Temperature Dependence of Halogenation 141
4-14 Halogenation of Higher Alkanes 142
4-15 The Hammond Postulate 148
    Problem Solving: Proposing Reaction Mechanisms 150
4-16 Reactive Intermediates 152

5 ALKYL HALIDES: NUCLEOPHILIC SUBSTITUTION AND ELIMINATION

164

5-1 Introduction 164
5-2 Nomenclature of Alkyl Halides 165
5-3 Common Uses of Alkyl Halides 167
5-4 Structure of Alkyl Halides 169
5-5 Physical Properties of Alkyl Halides 170

5-6   Preparation of Alkyl Halides 172
5-7   Reactions of Alkyl Halides: Substitution and Elimination 175
5-8   Second-Order Nucleophilic Substitution: The S_N2 Reaction 176
5-9   Stereochemistry of the S_N2 Reaction 178
5-10   Generality of the S_N2 Reaction 179
5-11   Structural Effects on the S_N2 Reaction 180
5-12   Strength of the Nucleophile in S_N2 Reactions 182
5-13   Steric Effects on Nucleophilicity 185
5-14   Leaving-Group Effects 185
5-15   First-Order Nucleophilic Substitution: The S_N1 Reaction 187
5-16   Stereochemistry of the S_N1 Reaction 191
5-17   Rearrangements in the S_N1 Reaction 192
5-18   Comparison of S_N1 and S_N2 Reactions 194
5-19   First-Order Elimination: The E1 Reaction 196
5-20   Second-Order Elimination: The E2 Reaction 198
5-21   Stereochemistry of the E2 Reaction 199
5-22   Positional Orientation of Elimination: The Saytzeff Rule 203
5-23   Comparison of E1 and E2 Elimination Mechanisms 205
5-24   Elimination Versus Substitution 206
5-25   Reduction of Alkyl Halides 208
       Problem Solving: Organic Synthesis 212

6 STEREOCHEMISTRY   223

6-1   Introduction 223
6-2   Chirality 224
6-3   (R) and (S) Nomenclature of Chiral Carbon Atoms 230
6-4   Optical Activity 234
6-5   Biological Discrimination of Enantiomers 240
6-6   Racemic Mixtures 241
6-7   Enantiometric Excess and Optical Purity 242
6-8   Chirality of Conformationally Mobile Systems 243
6-9   Chiral Compounds without Chiral Carbon Atoms 245
6-10   Fischer Projections 247
6-11   Diastereomers 252
6-12   Stereochemistry of Molecules with Two or More Chiral Carbon Atoms 255
6-13   Meso Compounds 256
6-14   Physical Properties of Diastereomers 258
6-15   Resolution of Enantiomers 259
6-16   Absolute and Relative Configuration 262
6-17   Reactions at the Chiral Carbon Atom: S_N1 and S_N2 Mechanisms 264
6-18   Reactions That Do Not Involve a Chiral Carbon Atom 267
6-19   Reactions That Generate a New Chiral Carbon Atom 267
6-20   Stereospecificity of Anti Eliminations 269

7 STRUCTURE AND SYNTHESIS OF ALKENES   277

7-1   Introduction 277
7-2   The Orbital Description of the Alkene Double Bond 278
7-3   Elements of Unsaturation 279

7-4   Nomenclature of Alkenes   282
7-5   Nomenclature of Geometric Isomers   283
7-6   Commercial Importance of Alkenes   286
7-7   Stability of Alkenes   286
7-8   Physical Properties of Alkenes   293
7-9   Synthesis of Alkenes   295
       Problem Solving: Proposing Reaction Mechanisms   301

8 REACTIONS OF ALKENES

                                                                          313

8-1   Reactivity of the Carbon-Carbon Double Bond   313
8-2   Electrophilic Addition to Alkenes   314
8-3   Addition of Hydrogen Halides to Alkenes   315
8-4   Addition of Water: Hydration of Alkenes   321
8-5   Indirect Hydration of Alkenes   323
8-6   Alkoxymercuration-Demercuration   326
8-7   Hydroboration of Alkenes   328
8-8   Catalytic Hydrogenation of Alkenes   333
8-9   Addition of Carbenes to Alkenes   334
8-10   Addition of Halogens to Alkenes   337
8-11   Formation of Halohydrins   339
8-12   Epoxidation of Alkenes   341
8-13   Acid-Catalyzed Opening of Epoxides   342
8-14   Syn Hydroxylation of Alkenes   344
8-15   Oxidative Cleavage of Alkenes   346
8-16   Dimerization and Polymerization of Alkenes   350

9 STRUCTURE AND SYNTHESIS OF ALCOHOLS

                                                                          364

9-1   Introduction   364
9-2   Structure and Classification of Alcohols   364
9-3   Nomenclature of Alcohols and Phenols   365
9-4   Physical Properties of Alcohols   370
9-5   Commercially Important Alcohols   372
9-6   Acidity of Alcohols and Phenols   374
9-7   Synthesis of Alcohols: Introduction and Review   377
9-8   Organometallic Reagents for Alcohol Synthesis   379
9-9   Addition of Organometallic Reagents to Carbonyl Compounds   381
9-10   Other Reactions of Organometallic Reagents: The Corey-House Reaction   386
9-11   Side Reactions of Organometallic Reagents   387
9-12   Reduction of the Carbonyl Group: Synthesis of Primary and Secondary Alcohols   389
9-13   Thiols (Mercaptans)   391

10 REACTIONS OF ALCOHOLS

                                                                             401

10-1   Oxidation States of Alcohols and Related Functional Groups   401
10-2   Oxidation of Alcohols   403
10-3   Additional Methods for Alcohol Oxidations   406

10-4   Biological Oxidation of Alcohols 407

10-5   Reduction of Alcohols 409

10-6   Alcohols as Nucleophiles and Electrophiles 410

10-7   Formation and Use of Tosylate Esters 410

10-8   Reactions of Alcohols with Hydrohalic Acids 412

10-9   Reactions of Alcohols with Phosphorus Halides 417

10-10   Reactions of Alcohols with Thionyl Chloride 418

10-11   Dehydration Reactions of Alcohols 420

10-12   Unique Reactions of Diols 424

Problem Solving: Proposing Reaction Mechanisms 424

10-13   Esterification of Alcohols 429

10-14   Esters of Inorganic Acids 430

10-15   Formation and Reactions of Alkoxides 432

Problem Solving: Multistep Synthesis 433

11   INFRARED SPECTROSCOPY AND MASS SPECTROMETRY   444

11-1   Introduction 444

11-2   The Electromagnetic Spectrum 445

11-3   The Infrared Region 447

11-4   Molecular Vibrations 447

11-5   IR-Active and IR-Inactive Vibrations 449

11-6   Measurement of the IR Spectrum 450

11-7   Infrared Spectroscopy of Hydrocarbons 452

11-8   Characteristic Absorptions of Alcohols and Amines 457

11-9   Characteristic Absorptions of Carbonyl Compounds 458

11-10   Characteristic Absorptions of Carbon-Nitrogen Bonds 463

11-11   Simplified Summary of IR Stretching Frequencies 465

11-12   Reading and Interpreting Infrared Spectra (Solved Problems) 467

11-13   Introduction to Mass Spectrometry 473

11-14   Determination of the Molecular Formula by Mass Spectrometry 476

11-15   Fragmentation Patterns in Mass Spectrometry 479

12   NUCLEAR MAGNETIC RESONANCE SPECTROSCOPY   490

12-1   Introduction 490

12-2   Theory of Nuclear Magnetic Resonance 490

12-3   Magnetic Shielding by Electrons 493

12-4   The NMR Spectrometer 495

12-5   The Chemical Shift 496

12-6   The Number of Signals 504

12-7   Areas of the Peaks 506

12-8   Spin-Spin Splitting 509

Problem Solving: Drawing an NMR Spectrum 515

12-9   Stereochemical Nonequivalence of Protons 524

12-10   Time Dependence of NMR Spectroscopy 526

12-11   Interpretation of Proton NMR Spectra 530

12-12   Carbon-13 NMR Spectroscopy 536

12-13   Interpretation of Carbon NMR Spectra 542
12-14   Strategy for Solving Spectral Problems 545

13 ETHERS AND EPOXIDES

559

13-1   Introduction 559
13-2   Physical Properties of Ethers 560
13-3   Nomenclature of Ethers 563
13-4   Spectroscopy of Ethers 567
13-5   The Williamson Ether Synthesis 569
13-6   Synthesis of Ethers by Alkoxymercuration-Demercuration 570
13-7   Synthesis of Ethers by Bimolecular Dehydration of Alcohols (Industrial Method) 571
13-8   Cleavage of Ethers by HBr and HI 572
13-9   Autoxidation of Ethers 574
13-10 Synthesis of Epoxides 575
13-11 Acid-Catalyzed Ring Opening of Epoxides 577
13-12 Base-Catalyzed Ring Opening of Epoxides 580
13-13 Orientation of Epoxide Ring Opening 581
13-14 Reactions of Grignard and Organolithium Reagents with Epoxides 583

14 ALKYNES

592

14-1   Introduction 592
14-2   Nomenclature of Alkynes 593
14-3   Electronic Structure of Alkynes 594
14-4   Physical Properties of Alkynes 595
14-5   Commercial Importance of Alkynes 595
14-6   Spectroscopy of Alkynes 597
14-7   Acidity of Alkynes 598
14-8   Synthesis of Alkynes from Acetylides 601
14-9   Synthesis of Alkynes by Elimination Reactions 604
14-10 Addition Reactions of Alkynes 607
14-11 Oxidation of Alkynes 615
        Problem Solving: Multistep Synthesis 617

15 CONJUGATED SYSTEMS ORBITAL SYMMETRY, AND ULTRAVIOLET SPECTROSCOPY

629

15-1   Introduction 629
15-2   Stabilities of Dienes 630
15-3   Molecular Orbital Picture of a Conjugated System 631
15-4   Allylic Cations 636
15-5   1,2- and 1,4-Addition to Conjugated Dienes 637
15-6   Kinetic Versus Thermodynamic Control in the Addition of HBR
           to 1,3-Butadiene 638
15-7   Allylic Radicals 640
15-8   Molecular Orbitals of the Allylic System 643
15-9   Electronic Configurations of the Allyl Radical, Cation, and Anion 644

15-10 S$_N$2 Displacement Reactions of Allylic Halides and Tosylates 646
15-11 The Diels-Alder Reaction 647
15-12 The Diels-Alder as an Example of a Pericyclic Reaction 655
15-13 Ultraviolet Absorption Spectroscopy 658

16 AROMATIC COMPOUNDS 672

16-1 Introduction; The Discovery of Benzene 672
16-2 The Structure and Properties of Benzene 672
16-3 The Molecular Orbitals of Benzene 677
16-4 The Molecular Orbital Picture of Cyclobutadiene 680
16-5 Aromatic, Antiaromatic, and Nonaromatic Compounds 682
16-6 Hückel's Rule 683
16-7 Molecular Orbital Derivation of Hückel's Rule 685
16-8 Aromatic Ions 686
16-9 Heterocyclic Aromatic Compounds 692
16-10 Polynuclear Aromatic Hydrocarbons 695
16-11 Fused Heterocyclic Compounds 697
16-12 Nomenclature of Benzene Derivatives 698
16-13 Physical Properties of Benzene and Its Derivatives 700
16-14 Spectroscopy of Aromatic Compounds 701

17 REACTIONS OF AROMATIC COMPOUNDS 715

17-1 Electrophilic Aromatic Substitution 715
17-2 Halogenation of Benzene 716
17-3 Nitration of Benzene 719
17-4 Sulfonation of Benzene 720
17-5 Nitration of Toluene: The Effect of Alkyl Substitution 721
17-6 Activating, Ortho, Para-Directing Substituents 724
17-7 Deactivating, Meta-Directing Substituents 727
17-8 Halogen Substituents: Deactivating, but Ortho, Para-Directing 731
17-9 Effects of More Than One Substituent on Electrophilic Aromatic Substitution 733
17-10 The Friedel-Crafts Alkylation 735
17-11 The Friedel-Crafts Acylation 740
17-12 Nucleophilic Aromatic Substitution 744
17-13 Addition Reactions of Benzene Derivatives 748
17-14 Side-Chain Reactions of Benzene Derivatives 751
17-15 Reactions of Phenols 755

18 KETONES AND ALDEHYDES 767

18-1 Carbonyl Compounds 767
18-2 Structure of the Carbonyl Group 768
18-3 Nomenclature of Ketones and Aldehydes 769
18-4 Physical Properties of Ketones and Aldehydes 771
18-5 Spectroscopy of Ketones and Aldehydes 773
18-6 Industrial Importance of Ketones and Aldehydes 781

18-7   Review of Synthesis of Ketones and Aldehydes 782
18-8   Synthesis of Ketones and Aldehydes Using 1,3-Dithianes 784
18-9   Synthesis of Ketones from Carboxylic Acids 785
18-10 Synthesis of Ketones from Nitriles 786
18-11 Synthesis of Aldehydes from Acid Chlorides 787
18-12 Reactions of Ketones and Aldehydes: Nucleophilic Addition 790
18-13 Nucleophilic Addition of Carbanions and Hydride Reagents (Review) 792
18-14 Nucleophilic Addition of Water: Hydration of Ketones and Aldehydes 794
18-15 Nucleophilic Addition of Hydrogen Cyanide: Formation of Cyanohydrins 795
18-16 Condensations with Ammonia and Primary Amines: Formation of Imines 797
18-17 Condensations with Hydroxylamine and Hydrazines 799
18-18 Nucleophilic Addition of Alcohols: Formation of Acetals 801
       Problem Solving: Proposing Reaction Mechanisms 803
18-19 Use of Acetals as Protecting Groups 806
18-20 Oxidation of Aldehydes 807
18-21 Deoxygenation of Ketones and Aldehydes 808

19   AMINES

823

19-1   Introduction 823
19-2   Nomenclature of Amines 825
19-3   Structure of Amines 827
19-4   Physical Properties of Amines 828
19-5   Spectroscopy of Amines 830
19-6   Basicity of Amines 835
19-7   Effects on Basicity of Amines 836
19-8   Salts of Amines 839
19-9   Amine Salts as Phase-Transfer Catalysts 840
19-10 Reactions of Amines with Ketones and Aldehydes 842
19-11 Aromatic Substitution of Aryl and Heterocyclic Amines 842
19-12 Alkylation of Amines by Alkyl Halides 846
19-13 Acylation of Amines by Acid Chlorides 848
19-14 Reaction of Amines with Sulfonyl Chlorides; Sulfonamides 849
19-15 Amines As Leaving Groups; The Hofmann Elimination 850
19-16 Oxidation of Amines; The Cope Elimination 853
19-17 Reactions of Amines with Nitrous Acid 855
19-18 Formation and Reactions of Arenediazonium Salts 857
19-19 Synthesis of Amines by Reductive Amination 865
19-20 Synthesis of Amines by Acylation-Reduction 866
19-21 Reduction of Nitro Compounds; Synthesis of Arylamines 868
19-22 Direct Alkylation of Ammonia and Amines 869
19-23 The Gabriel Synthesis of Primary Amines 870
19-24 Reduction of Nitriles to Primary Amines 871
19-25 The Hofmann Rearrangement of Amides 872

20   CARBOXYLIC ACIDS

887

20-1   Introduction 887
20-2   Nomenclature of Carboxylic Acids 888
20-3   Physical Properties of Carboxylic Acids 891
20-4   Acidity of Carboxylic Acids 892

20-5 Salts of Carboxylic Acids 895
20-6 Commercial Sources of Carboxylic Acids 898
20-7 Spectroscopy of Carboxylic Acids 899
20-8 Synthesis of Carboxylic Acids 903
20-9 Reactions of Carboxylic Acids and Their Derivatives; Nucleophilic Acyl Substitution 907
20-10 Synthesis and Use of Acid Chlorides 908
20-11 Condensation of Acids with Alcohols: The Fischer Esterification 910
20-12 Esterification Using Diazomethane 911
20-13 Condensation of Acids with Amines: Direct Synthesis of Amides 912
20-14 Reduction of Carboxylic Acids 913
20-15 Alkylation of Carboxylic Acids to Form Ketones 914
20-16 Decarboxylation of Carboxylate Radicals: The Hunsdiecker Reaction 915

21 CARBOXYLIC ACID DERIVATIVES 926

21-1 Introduction 926
21-2 Structure and Nomenclature of Acid Derivatives 926
21-3 Physical Properties of Carboxylic Acid Derivatives 933
21-4 Spectroscopy of Carboxylic Acid Derivatives 935
21-5 Interconversion of Acid Derivatives by Nucleophilic Acyl Substitution 943
21-6 Acid-Catalyzed Nucleophilic Acyl Substitution 949
   Problem Solving: Proposing Reaction Mechanisms 949
21-7 Hydrolysis of Carboxylic Acid Derivatives 951
21-8 Reduction of Acid Derivatives 955
21-9 Reactions of Acid Derivatives with Organometallic Reagents 958
21-10 Overview of the Chemistry of Acid Chlorides 959
21-11 Overview of the Chemistry of Anhydrides 961
21-12 Overview of the Chemistry of Esters 964
21-13 Overview of the Chemistry of Amides 966
21-14 Overview of the Chemistry of Nitriles 969
21-15 Thioesters 970
21-16 Esters and Amides of Carbonic Acid 971

22 ADDITIONS AND CONDENSATIONS OF ENOLS AND ENOLATE IONS 984

22-1 Introduction 984
22-2 α Halogenation of Ketones 989
22-3 α Bromination of Acids (The HVZ Reaction) 993
22-4 Alkylation of Enolate Ions 994
22-5 Formation and Alkylation of Enamines 995
22-6 The Aldol Condensation of Ketones and Aldehydes 998
22-7 Dehydration of Aldol Products 1000
22-8 Crossed Aldol Condensations 1001
   Problem Solving: Proposing Reaction Mechanisms 1003
22-9 Aldol Cyclizations 1005
22-10 Planning Syntheses Using Aldol Condensations 1006
22-11 The Cannizzaro Reaction 1007
22-12 The Wittig Reaction 1009

22-13 The Claisen Ester Condensation 1012
22-14 The Dieckmann Condensation: A Claisen Cyclization 1016
22-15 Crossed Claisen Condensations 1017
22-16 Condensations Using a Temporary Ester Group 1020
22-17 The Malonic Ester Synthesis 1021
22-18 The Acetoacetic Ester Synthesis 1023
22-19 Conjugate Additions: The Michael Reaction 1026
22-20 The Robinson Annulation 1029
Problem Solving: Proposing Reaction Mechanisms 1030

23 CARBOHYDRATES AND NUCLEIC ACIDS
1043

23-1 Introduction 1043
23-2 Classification of Carbohydrates 1044
23-3 Monosaccharides 1045
23-4 Erythro and Threo Diastereomers 1048
23-5 Epimers 1049
23-6 Cyclic Structures of Monosaccharides 1050
23-7 Anomers of Monosaccharides; Mutarotation 1054
23-8 Reactions of Monosaccharides: Side Reactions in Base 1057
23-9 Reduction of Monosaccharides 1059
23-10 Oxidation of Monosaccharides; Reducing Sugars 1059
23-11 Nonreducing Sugars: Formation of Glycosides 1061
23-12 Ether and Ester Formation 1064
23-13 Reactions with Phenylhydrazine: Osozone Formation 1066
23-14 Chain Shortening: The Ruff Degradation 1067
23-15 Chain Lengthening: The Kiliani-Fischer Synthesis 1068
23-16 Fischer's Proof of the Configuration of Glucose 1072
23-17 Determination of Ring Size; Periodic Acid Cleavage of Sugars 1075
23-18 Disaccharides 1077
23-19 Polysaccharides 1082
23-20 Nucleic Acids: Introduction 1086
23-21 Ribonucleosides and Ribonucleotides 1087
23-22 The Bonding Structure of Ribonucleic Acid 1089
23-23 Deoxyribose and the Structure of Deoxyribonucleic Acid 1090

24 AMINO ACIDS, PEPTIDES, AND PROTEINS
1101

24-1 Introduction 1101
24-2 Structure and Stereochemistry of the α-Amino Acids 1102
24-3 Acid-Base Properties of Amino Acids 1106
24-4 Isoelectric Points and Electrophoresis 1107
24-5 Synthesis of Amino Acids 1110
24-6 Resolution of Amino Acids 1114
24-7 Reactions of Amino Acids 1115
24-8 Structure and Nomenclature of Peptides and Proteins 1118
24-9 Peptide Structure Determination 1122
24-10 Classical Peptide Synthesis 1128

24-11 Solid-Phase Peptide Synthesis 1131
24-12 Classification of Proteins 1135
24-13 Levels of Protein Structure 1136
24-14 Protein Denaturation 1139

25 LIPIDS   1146

25-1 Introduction 1146
25-2 Waxes 1146
25-3 Triglycerides 1147
25-4 Saponification of Fats and Oils: Soaps and Detergents 1150
25-5 Phospholipids 1153
25-6 Steroids 1155
25-7 Prostaglandins 1158
25-8 Terpenes 1159

26 SYNTHETIC POLYMERS   1166

26-1 Introduction 1166
26-2 Addition Polymers 1167
26-3 Stereochemistry of Polymers 1173
26-4 Stereochemical Control of Polymerization: Ziegler-Natta Catalysts 1174
26-5 Natural and Synthetic Rubbers 1175
26-6 Copolymers of Two or More Monomers 1177
26-7 Condensation Polymers 1177
26-8 Polymer Structure and Properties 1181

APPENDICES   1187

1A NMR Absorption Positions of Protons in Various Structural Environments 1188
1B Spin-spin Coupling Constants 1189
2A Characteristic Infrared Group Frequencies 1190
2B Characteristic Infrared Absorptions of Functional Groups 1193
3   The Woodward-Fieser Rules for Predicting Ultraviolet-Visible Spectra 1195
4A Methods and Suggestions for Proposing Mechanisms 1199
4B Suggestions for Developing Multistep Syntheses 1202
4C Suggestions for Drawing a Proposed NMR Spectrum 1203

ANSWERS TO SELECTED PROBLEMS 1204

INDEX 1213

PREFACE

Organic chemistry students are often overwhelmed by the number of compounds, names, reactions, and mechanisms that confront them. They wonder whether they can learn all this material in a single year. Perhaps the most important function of a textbook is to organize the material to show students that most of organic chemistry consists of a few basic principles and a large number of extensions and applications of these principles. Relatively little memorization is required if the student grasps each major concept and develops flexibility in applying that concept.

In writing the first edition, my goal was to produce a modern, readable text that uses the most effective techniques of presentation and review. This second edition extends and refines that goal, differing from the first edition in several respects:

1. The chapters are reorganized to place stereochemistry and spectroscopy earlier, with these topics then integrated into all the functional group chapters.

2. Several topics have been added or have received increased emphasis in this edition. For example, sections on periodic acid cleavage of glycols and DIBAH reduction of esters have been added. Phenols, quinones, and thiols are a few of the topics that have received increased emphasis.

3. A number of new features have been added, including about a dozen problem-solving discussions, summary tables for comparing and contrasting important concepts, additional spectroscopy problems, and appendices on nomenclature, problem solving, and UV spectroscopy.

The entire book has been extensively microedited to tighten up the style and ensure clarity. In some cases, redundant examples have been eliminated. The chapters on stereochemistry have received particular attention, having been combined from two chapters into one. Similarly, the two chapters covering carboxylic acid derivatives have been combined into one, and most of the chemistry is now presented by reaction type (comparing the reactivity of the different acid derivatives) rather than one acid derivative at a time.

As in the first edition, each new topic is introduced carefully and explained thoroughly. Whenever possible, illustrations are used to help the student visualize each physical concept, and many in-chapter problems give immediate reinforcement as the student works through each chapter.

Throughout the book, the emphasis is on *chemical reactivity*. Chemical reactions are introduced as soon as possible, and each functional group is considered in view of its reactivity toward electrophiles, nucleophiles, oxidants, reductants, and other reagents. "Electron-pushing" mechanisms are stressed throughout as a means of explaining and predicting this reactivity. Structural concepts such as stereochemistry and spectroscopy are thoroughly covered as well, but they are presented as useful techniques that enhance the fundamental study of chemical reactivity.

This book maintains the traditional organization that concentrates on one functional group at a time while comparing and contrasting the reactivity of different functional groups. Reactions are emphasized beginning in Chapter 4. Most of the important substitution, addition, and elimination reactions appear before the other major theory and structure chapters.

Some stereospecific substitutions and eliminations are first encountered before the stereochemistry chapter. These reactions are initially discussed using examples in which stereochemical changes are apparent from the cis or trans arrangement of substituents on a ring or double bond. When chiral compounds and nongeometric diastereomers are introduced in Chapter 6, stereospecific reactions are reviewed using these compounds as examples. This organization helps students learn these difficult topics by first emphasizing the reactions using simple examples and concentrating on reactivity. More esoteric stereochemical examples are used later as a review, once stereochemistry has been covered in detail.

Spectroscopy appears earlier in this edition than it did in the first. Spectroscopic techniques (IR, MS, and NMR) are covered in Chapters 11 and 12, where they will be encountered in the first semester. Still, a large amount of organic chemistry has been covered before this digression into structure determination. The principles of spectroscopy are reinforced in later chapters, where the characteristic spectral features of each functional group are summarized and representative spectroscopy problems appear.

FLEXIBILITY OF COVERAGE

No two instructors teach organic chemistry in exactly the same way. This book covers all the fundamental topics in detail, building each new concept on those that come before. Many topics may be given more or less emphasis at the discretion of the instructor. Examples of these topics are ^{13}C NMR spectroscopy, ultraviolet spectroscopy, conservation of orbital symmetry, nucleic acids, and the special topics chapters: lipids and synthetic polymers.

Another area of flexibility is in the problems. The wide-ranging problem sets review the material from several viewpoints, and more study problems are provided than most students would be able to complete. This large variety allows the instructor to select the most appropriate problems for the individual course.

UP-TO-DATE TREATMENT

In addition to the classical reactions, this book covers many techniques and reactions that have more recently gained wide use among practicing chemists. Molecular-orbital theory is introduced early and used to explain electronic effects in conjugated and aromatic systems, pericyclic reactions, and ultraviolet spectroscopy. Carbon-13 NMR spectroscopy is treated as the routine tool it has become in most research laboratories. Many of the newer synthetic techniques are also included, such as the Birch reduction, DIBAH reduction of esters, alkylation of 1,3-dithianes, and oxidations using pyridinium chlorochromate.

REACTION MECHANISMS

Reaction mechanisms are important in all areas of organic chemistry, but they are difficult for many students. Students fall into the trap of memorizing a mechanism